A Gift for

_____

Presented by

_____

i before e
(except after c)

The Young Readers Edition

i before e
(except after c)

Easy, Cool Ways to
Remember Facts

Susan Randol

Reader's
Digest

The Reader's Digest Association, Inc.
New York, NY / Montreal

A READER'S DIGEST BOOK

Copyright © 2012 Reader's Digest

All rights reserved. Unauthorized reproduction, in any manner, is prohibited.

Reader's Digest is a registered trademark of The Reader's Digest Association, Inc.

Illustrations by Andrew Pinder

READER'S DIGEST TRADE PUBLISHING

U.S. Project Editor: Rebecca Behan

Manager, English Book Editorial, Reader's Digest Canada: Pamela Johnson

Project Production Coordinator: Nick Anderson

Senior Art Director: George McKeon

Executive Editor, Trade Publishing: Dolores York

Associate Publisher, Trade Publishing: Rosanne McManus

President and Publisher, Trade Publishing: Harold Clarke

Library of Congress Cataloging in Publication Data

Randol, Susan.
  I before e (except after c) : easy, cool ways to remember facts / Susan Randol.
      p. cm.
  "A Reader's Digest Book."
  Includes bibliographical references and index.
  ISBN 978-1-60652-348-3
  1. Mnemonics--Juvenile literature. I. Title.
  BF385.R26 2012
  153.1'4--dc23

                          2011026579

Reader's Digest is committed to both the quality of our products and the service we provide
to our customers. We value your comments, so please feel free to contact us:

      The Reader's Digest Association, Inc.

      Adult Trade Publishing

      44 S. Broadway

      White Plains, NY 10601

For more Reader's Digest products and information, visit our website:

      www.rd.com (in the United States)

      www.readersdigest.ca (in Canada)

Printed in the United States of America

3 5 7 9 10 8 6 4 2

For Diana and Ellen

CONTENTS

START HERE!

Think about all the stuff you have to remember every day. You have to remember to feed your pets, take your lunch to school, write down homework assignments, bring textbooks home for studying, practice your instrument, and more and more and more. But this list of things to remember doesn't even begin to include all the information you have to remember for tests and quizzes and papers. What to do?

Start with this book! It's filled with tricks that help you remember all the stuff you need to know. These tricks—called mnemonics (ditch the *m* when you pronounce the word)—are like sticky notes for your brain. You can use them to remember how many days are in the month of March, the names of the planets, the difference between longitude and latitude, the correct spelling of *attendance* (or is it spelled *attendence*?), the seven wonders of the ancient world, the three types of angles in geometry, the different sections found in an orchestra, and so much more.

Best of all, these tricks are fun! On the following page you'll find three main kinds of memory tricks.

Acronyms These are words formed from the first letter (or letters) of a series of words, like USA (**U**nited **S**tates of **A**merica), radar (**Ra**dio **D**etection **A**nd **R**anging), and NASA (**N**ational **A**eronautics and **S**pace **A**dministration). Acronyms help you remember short phrases easily.

Acrostics The first letter of each word in an acrostic sentence is the first letter of what you need to remember. Acrostics are really helpful when you need to remember a list of items. For example, if you need to remember the names of the countries in Central America, you just need to learn this acrostic sentence: **M**y **B**ig **G**erbil **E**ats **H**is **N**ew **C**arrots **P**olitely. That's a lot easier to remember than Mexico, Belize, Guatemala, El Salvador, Honduras, Nicaragua, Costa Rica, and Panama!

Rhymes Whether they're simple poems or songs with many verses, rhymes get stuck in your head—and make information easy to remember. The title of this book comes from one of the most popular mnemonic rhymes:

> *i* before *e,* except after *c*
> Or when sounding like *a*
> As in *neighbor* and *weigh.*

You'll also discover occasional puns and other words used playfully to help you store information in your brain. For example, you'll know how to change your clock for daylight savings time if you remember "spring forward, fall back." Pictures scattered throughout these pages will help you remember bits of information too.

Finally, you'll see two kinds of boxes: Extra Credit boxes ask you to make up your own mnemonic devices or answer quirky questions based on the mnemonics you've just learned, and the boxes called Too Cool for School give you fun facts and amazing information you can use to impress your family and friends.

So check out these fun, clever, and often silly ways to memorize the tons of stuff you have to remember every day. You may surprise your parents and teachers—and even yourself—with what you learn!

DAYS AND NIGHTS

Thirty days hath September...

CLOCKS AND CALENDARS

Have you ever heard someone say, "Time marches on?" You might get a funny picture in your head of a clock with legs, or you might think about how seasons change or about how the same time can be different in two places. There's a lot to learn about time—and a lot to remember. So kick that walking clock out of your head, and make room for some fun time-related mnemonics.

What a Quirky Calendar!

You learned the days of the week and the months of the year a long, long time ago. If you try really hard, you can probably recite them backward! But some parts of the calendar aren't so easy to learn and are even harder to remember. Quick: how many days does March have? If you don't know, you can use a version of this classic rhyme to help you. The first version is the easiest (and silliest, since the last two lines don't even rhyme!).

> Thirty days hath September,
> April, June, and November;
> All the rest have thirty-one
> Except for February, which has twenty-eight.

Then there are variations on that classic poem:

> Thirty days hath September,
> April, June, and November;
> All the rest have thirty-one
> Excepting February alone.

And if you want to include leap years—when a day is added to February every four years—just add these two lines to your poem:

> And that has twenty-eight days clear,
> With twenty-nine in each leap year.

Or just try out this entire poem:

> Thirty days hath September,
> April, June, and November;
> All the rest have thirty-one

Except February, my dear son.
It has twenty-eight and that is fine,
But in leap year it has twenty-nine.

And Speaking of Leap Years . . .

Have you ever had a friend you thought was your age who turned out to have had only three birthdays? Or four? It could happen! If your friend was born on February 29 in a leap year, he wouldn't have a birthday every year like you, since February 29 comes around only once every four years. He'd have a birthday every four years instead. So if you (born on any day except February 29) and your friend were born in 2008, by 2012 (the next leap year) you'd have celebrated four birthdays, but he'd have celebrated only one! And in 2016, you'd have had eight birthdays but he'd have had only two! How can you keep track of which year is a leap year? Use your four times table. Start with a recent leap year—say, 2008—and go from there.

More about Months

If you learn faster by *looking* at what you have to memorize, you can use your hands to teach you the number of days in each month.

Clench your fists, and hold them out in front of you. Each knuckle stands for a month with thirty-one days, and each valley between knuckles stands for a month with thirty days (except February). Starting with the knuckle on your left hand, name the months in order, moving from knuckle to valley: January (knuckle = 31 days), February (valley = 28 days), March (knuckle = 31 days), April (valley = 30 days), and so on. Don't count your thumb knuckles, and don't forget that February likes to mess everything up with only twenty-eight days (or 29 in a leap year).

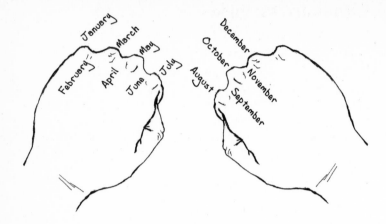

Changing Seasons and Time

What if you could add an extra hour of daylight to summer days so you could play with your friends outside just a little big longer? In a way, you can. Every March, daylight savings time begins. This means you set your clocks forward one hour (so 4:00 in the afternoon becomes 5:00 p.m., for example). You don't really get an extra hour (since 12:00 midnight becomes 1:00 a.m. the next day), but you do get to enjoy more sunlight during waking hours. Then in the fall, you reset your clocks back one hour, so 5:00 in the afternoon becomes 4:00 p.m. How can you remember which way to turn your clock's hands? Easy. In the **spring** you move your clock one hour **forward,** and in the **fall** you set your clock **back** one hour:

Spring forward, fall back.

Or, if you prefer a simple rhyme, try this:

Forward March, back November,
That is all you must remember!

Travel Time Machine

You're standing in California at 1:00 p.m. and you want to go to New York. You take a time machine since a plane will take too long. Even though the time machine got you to New York in one second, you discover that it's already 4:00 p.m. on the East Coast. You lost three hours! When you travel from west to east anywhere in the world you lose time. When you travel from east to west you gain time. Remember it this way:

West to **E**ast **L**oses; **E**ast to **W**est **G**ains.

Imagine:

We **E**njoy **L**ollipops; **E**veryone **W**ants **G**um.

We **E**at **L**emons; **E**veryone **W**ants **G**rapes.

> ### EXTRA CREDIT
> *Try coming up with your own sentence for "West to East Loses; East to West Gains." Make it really memorable by using the word* **giraffe.**

Changing Seasons

You know that winter really starts when the first snow falls and summer really begins when school ends. But the calendar likes to be a little more precise than that. Say this sentence to remember when each season begins:

Twenty soldiers **March** through **three** other seasons.

How does it work? Start with **March**, when spring starts, around the **twentieth** (depending on the year). Every

other season starts **three** months after the one before it: March (spring starts), June (summer starts), September (fall starts), and December (winter starts). Picture twenty soldiers marching through the pages of a calendar, and you'll never forget when each season begins.

Foul Weather Ahead

Whether you live in a state that gets hit by hurricanes or you're planning to visit a place that hurricanes like to visit too, you need to know when to look out for them. Here are the five months when you should be on high alert:

June—too soon (for a big, bad storm)

July—stand by (because it could arrive)

August—you must (be prepared for the big one)

September—remember (that the season is still going strong)

October—all over (until June)

THE SKY

Ancient people used the moon, the sun, and planets to create their calendar, so it makes sense to talk about the sky when we're talking about the calendar.

But remembering the order of the planets in the solar system, which planets are the biggest (and the smallest), and which stars are the brightest may seem a lot harder than remembering how many days are in a month. You'll be able to remember everything you need to know about the sky, though, if you use these tricks.

Planets in the Solar System

Astronomers used to believe that there were nine planets in our solar system.

Mercury

Venus

Earth

Mars

Jupiter

Saturn

Uranus

Neptune

Pluto

And remembering their order—starting at the sun and moving out to the edge of the solar system, as in the list above—was easy, as long as you could remember this classic sentence:

My **V**ery **E**ducated **M**other **J**ust **S**erved **U**s **N**ine **P**izzas.

If you don't like pizza, you can also say that your mother served you **P**eanuts, **P**ickles, or **P**eas.

Another sentence that's easy to remember (and actually makes more sense) is:

My **V**ery **E**ducated **M**other **J**ust **S**howed **U**s **N**ine **P**lanets.

But wait! In 2006, the International Astronomical Union demoted Pluto from planet to dwarf planet, so everybody had to learn a new way to memorize the order. Take the **P** off the end of the sentence and what do you have left?

My **V**ery **E**ducated **M**other **J**ust **S**erved **U**s **N**achos.

... or **N**oodles or **N**uts or **N**ectarines.

Better yet, try a loony sentence like this:

My **V**ery **E**ccentric **M**other **J**ust **S**erved **U**s **N**aked!

> ### EXTRA CREDIT
> *Write your own sentence that helps you remember the order of the planets. Try one with the word **evil** in it.*

Planets in Order of Size

Teachers aren't always happy once you know the order of planets in the solar system—they want you to know the planets in order of size, too! From smallest to largest (including Pluto) they are:

Pluto

Mercury

Mars

Venus

Earth

Neptune

Uranus

Saturn

Jupiter

That's a lot to remember, especially after you memorized the planets in another order already. Make up a particularly nutty acrostic so you don't confuse the two.

Playful **M**artians **M**ake **V**ery **E**xcited **N**oises **U**ntil **S**omeone **J**udges.

Get rid of *Playful* and start with *Martians* if you don't want to remember Pluto (though don't you feel a little sorry for that little planet?).

You can show off how much you know about planets by reciting them in order of size from largest to smallest:

Jupiter

Saturn

Uranus

Neptune

Earth

Venus

Mars

Mercury

Pluto

Just remember this:

Jane **S**ulks **U**nless **N**early **E**veryone **V**isits **M**y **M**other's **P**arrot.

And you can easily drop Pluto here too:

Jane **S**ulks **U**nless **N**early **E**veryone **V**isits **M**y **M**other.

> ## TOO COOL FOR SCHOOL
> *Jupiter is so big that all the other planets could fit inside it.*

Rocky Planets, Gas Planets

If you're a very advanced student, you might have heard of rocky planets and gas planets.

Rocky planets are also called terrestrial planets. They are made up of material like that of the Earth, are small compared to the other planets, and are the planets closest to the sun. The rocky planets are:

Mercury

Venus

Earth

Mars

Just think:

My **V**ampire **E**ats **M**eat.

My **V**ampire **E**xpects **M**usic.

Gas planets have rings and moons, and (big surprise!) are primarily made up of gases. They are the planets farthest from the sun.

Jupiter

Saturn

Uranus

Neptune

Remember these acrostics:

Just **S**tay **U**ntil **N**oon.

Jack **S**ays **U**nicorns **N**eigh.

Moon Walk

Lots of people might be able to do the moonwalk dance move, but only twelve men have ever actually walked on the moon. Who was the first? Neil Armstrong, on July 20, 1969. He and two other astronauts made up the crew of Apollo 11, which flew them to the moon.

Remembering the astronauts on that mission is as easy as remembering your **ABC**s.

Neil **A**rmstrong

Buzz Aldrin

Michael **C**ollins

And remembering the number of the Apollo spacecraft is even easier than remembering your 123s: just replace the *l*s in the word *Apollo* with 1s, and you'll never forget Apollo 11.

TOO COOL FOR SCHOOL
The Apollo space program was named after the Greek god of the sun.

Star Light, Star Bright

The sun is the closest star to Earth and the brightest star in the sky, but the wishing rhyme you learned as a child doesn't make a lot of sense with *sun* in the poem:

> Sun light, sun bright,
> First sun I see tonight.
> I wish I may, I wish I might,
> Have the wish I wish tonight.

Maybe that's because the sun (obviously) isn't the brightest star *at night*. That award goes to Sirius, which is part of the group of stars (or constellation) called Canis Major.

These are the brightest nighttime stars visible from Earth—starting with the brightest of all—followed by the name of the constellation where each star is located:

Sirius in Canis Major

Canopeus in Carina

Rigil Kentaurus in Centaurus

Arcturus in Boötes

Vega in Lyra

Capella in Auriga

Rigel in Orion

Procyon in Canis Minor

Achernar in Eridanus

How can you remember all this? As long as you know that people used VCRs before DVD and BluRay players, you should be able to remember this sentence:

Sir Can Rig A VCR, PA.

TOO COOL FOR SCHOOL

Sirius is called the Dog Star because it is the brightest star in the constellation Canis Major, which means Greater Dog in Latin. And the expression "dog days of summer," those hot and lazy days when you're too tired to do anything, comes from Sirius too—the ancient Romans noticed that the star rose just before sunrise in the hottest part of the year.

Out of This World: the Earth's Atmospheres

Maybe you've heard someone say that the cost of something was in the stratosphere, meaning that it was very expensive—not that the price of the object literally was posted in the sky. But in fact the sky is exactly where you'll find the stratosphere, and where you'll find the earth's five atmospheres. Here they are, starting with the atmosphere closest to earth and ending with the one farthest away:

Troposphere
Stratosphere
Mesosphere
Thermosphere
Exosphere

Just remember:

The **S**hort **M**an **T**alks **E**ndlessly.
The **S**mall **M**ouse **T**ires **E**asily.

Even if you can't remember the exact names of each atmosphere (since they're kind of complicated), once you know the order you'll be able to recognize them when you see them.

Over the Rainbow

Just like planets and stars and atmospheres, the colors of the rainbow appear in a certain order:

Red

Orange

Yellow

Green

Blue

Indigo

Violet

You can always make up your own sentence to help you memorize the order, but it's much easier to remember this name:

ROY G BIV

EXTRA CREDIT
Can you make up an acrostic sentence that will help you remember the colors of the rainbow?

Using the Sky to Forecast the Weather

Long, long ago, before radar and satellites (and before you were born), people used what they saw in the sky to predict the weather. They remembered what to look for with clever little rhymes:

Red sky at night, sailor's delight;
Red sky at morning, sailors take warning.

(If sailors saw a red sky at night, the weather the next day would be fine for sailing; but if they saw a red sky in the morning, they should stay home!)

When clouds appear like rocks and towers,
The earth's refreshed by frequent showers.

A ring around the moon,
Means it'll rain soon.

Thunder in the morning,
All day storming.
Thunder at night,
Is the traveler's delight.

Rain before seven,
Dry by eleven.

OUR PLANET

Never Stop Eating Apples, Apples, Apples, Apples!

ALL ABOUT THE EARTH

Now it's time to get your head out of the clouds (from learning about planets and stars) and come down to Earth. You know there are lots of interesting facts about our planet, from the directions on a compass or the names of the Great Lakes or how to tell a stalactite from a stalagmite (and what are they, anyway?). Using memory tricks will definitely help you remember what you need to know.

Directions on a Map

Directions on a map or a compass will help you figure out where to go, as long as you can remember which direction is north or south or east or west.

You know that the top of the compass indicates north. Move around the compass clockwise—the way the hands of a clock move—and you'll pass east, south, and west before you return to north. Here's how to remember the order:

Never **E**at **S**hredded **W**heat.

But if you like shredded wheat, you can try the sentences on page 36 instead.

Nutty **E**lephants **S**wim **W**ildly.

Nobody **E**ver **S**aw **W**erewolves.

Latitude and Longitude

Mapmakers want you to know more than the directions on
the compass. They also want you to remember latitude and
longitude, which helps them (and you) find any location on
the Earth's surface.

The lines that run around the Earth are lines of latitude.
They are parallel lines of different lengths. The longest line
runs through the equator, the fattest part of the planet.
There are two easy ways to remember that lines of latitude
run around the earth's middle:

Lat is *fat* (the lines follow the equator, the fattest part of
the planet).

Lat is *flat* (the lines run horizontally, or from east to west).

The lines that run from the North Pole to the South Pole—which are all the same length—are lines of longitude. There are two ways to remember this too:

Longitude lines seem *long*er (because they stretch all the way from north to south).

Lo**N**gitude has an **N** in it, just like **N**orth Pole (since lines of longitude touch the North Pole).

The Continents

Sometimes you have to point out continents—the earth's seven large areas of land—on a map. The continents are:

North America

South America

Europe

Africa

Antarctica

Asia

Australia

The easiest way to remember them is by shouting:

Never **S**top **E**ating **A**pples, **A**pples, **A**pples, **A**pples!

You can also recite this poem called "The Seven Continents," by Amy Anderson:

To learn the seven continents,
Start with the letter A,
And when you're down to only one,
An E will save the day.

There's Africa, Antarctica, Australia, Asia, too.
The oceans run between them with their waters deep and blue.
There's also two Americas: North and South you see,
Now we're coming to the end,
Europe starts with E.

Maybe you want to remember the continents in order of size, from biggest to smallest:

Asia
Africa
North America
South America
Antarctica
Australia
Europe

Try remembering them this way:

Ask **Af**ter **N**ora; **S**he **An**gers **Au**nt **E**llen.

Oceans

Five oceans cover about seventy percent of the Earth with water. That's a lot of water—and a lot of oceans to remember. The oceans—from largest to smallest—are:

Pacific

Atlantic

Indian

Southern

Arctic

If you want to remember them in order, try calling upon the famous English physicist Sir Isaac Newton:

Point **A**t **I**saac's **S**wollen **A**nkles.

If you don't care about the order and just want to remember the names, you'll find these sentences easy on your brain:

I Ate **S**ome **A**pple **P**ie.

I Am **A S**illy **P**erson!

> **EXTRA CREDIT**
> *The Southern Ocean is also known as the Great Southern Ocean, the Antarctic Ocean, and the South Polar Ocean. Do you know anything else that has three other names?*

Biggest Islands

The three largest islands in the world are:

Greenland

New Guinea

Borneo

Can you come up with a clever way to remember them? You can always just say **GNB**, but that doesn't make any sense. Try creating a sentence to help you remember instead, like this one:

Go **N**uts, **B**obby!

The Great Lakes

The Great Lakes are so big that you generally can't see from one side to the other, just like an ocean! But they really are lakes, and you may need to remember their names—which is easy if you just think of **HOMES**:

Huron

Ontario

Michigan

Erie

Superior

But if you need to remember them in a certain order, you have to be a little more creative. Here they are in order from west to east:

Superior

Michigan

Huron

Erie

Ontario

Thinking about onions and oatmeal will help you remember them:

Sally's **M**other **H**ates **E**ating **O**nions.

Sam **M**ade **H**annah **E**at **O**atmeal.

EXTRA CREDIT
Think of an acrostic sentence that helps you remember the Great Lakes from east to west.

And if you have to list the Great Lakes according to size:

Superior
Huron
Michigan
Erie
Ontario

Picture this:

Scott's **H**orse **M**ust **E**at **O**ats.

Longest Rivers in the World

Now that you know the names of the oceans and the Great Lakes, you can think about more water—rivers. Nobody seems to agree on the order of the top ten longest rivers in the world, but most people agree on the top three:

Nile
Amazon
Yangtze

Sometimes the Mississippi-Missouri River is listed as the third longest river, but should it be? **NAY.**

If you add the Mississippi-Missouri River to the list, you can **NAY-M** (sound it out: *name*) them all easily.

Deserts

Now we'll go from wet—rivers and oceans—to very, very dry—deserts. But did you know that you can find penguins in the desert? The largest desert is actually in Antarctica, which gets less than ten inches of rain per year! But most people think of heat and camels and sand (rather than ice) when they think of deserts, so we'll stick with the biggest non-polar deserts. They are, in order of size:

Sahara

Arabian

Gobi

Their initials spell **SAG**.

> ### TOO COOL FOR SCHOOL
> *About one-third of the Earth's land is desert.*

Highest Mountains

The second tallest mountain in the world has a number in its name: two (K2). That's an easy way to remember that it's the *second* tallest, but how can you remember the rest?

Everest

K2

Kangchenjunga

Lhotse

Makalu

Try this:

Evan **K**icked **2 K**angaroos **L**ightly, **M**other.

It's hard to remember how to spell some of these mountains, but at least now you can put them in order of height if you see their names!

Stalagmites and Stalactites

Caves are really cool, and the things you can find inside them are pretty awesome too. If you look down in a limestone cave you might see stalagmites, cone-shaped formations growing from the floor upward. If you look up, you might see stalactites, icicle-shaped formations growing from the ceiling downward.

Even though these are tough words to say and to spell, they're not tough to remember.

Stala**G**mites are found on the **G**round.

Stala**C**tites are found on the **C**eiling.

Or you can remember that *mites* are little insects that crawl around on the *ground*, and *tights hang down* from a clothesline to dry.

Types of Rock

And no, we're not talking about music here. We're talking about the different types (or classes) of rocks that make up the outer solid layer of the earth. The three kinds are:

Metamorphic

Sedimentary

Igneous

As long as you don't mind spelling *said* wrong and using a fancy word that means "to set on fire," you can remember them this way:

Melanie **Sed Ign**ite!

WAY BACK WHEN

Just as you tell time with years, months, weeks, days, hours, minutes, and seconds, geologists tell time with eons, eras, periods, and epochs. Geological time is measured in millions of years—each eon consists of *hundreds of millions* of years!—so telling time in geology is a little bit different from figuring out how many hours a day you have to do homework.

Telling Time in Eras

The most recent eon—the Phanerozoic, also known as the age of visible life—is divided into three eras, which you may recognize:

> **Pa**leozoic (about 540 million years ago to 248 million years ago)
>
> **Me**sozoic (about 248 million years ago to 65 million years ago)
>
> **Ce**nozoic (about 65 million years ago to today)

Remember them (and their order) this way:

> **Pa**ss **Me Ce**real.

Or, if you want to remember them from most recent to longest ago, try this:

> **Ce**lebrate **Me**, **Pal!**

Telling Time in Periods

Each era is broken down into periods, and there are eleven main geological periods. The coolest periods are in the Mesozoic era, when dinosaurs ruled the Earth. Have you

first of three ages archaeologists use to classify prehistoric societies by their tools? The three stages are:

Stone Age
Bronze Age
Iron Age

Remember them using this acrostic:

Sam **B**ullies **I**van.

You can break the Stone Age down even further, if you want. It consists of three periods:

Paleolithic
Mesolithic
Neolithic

Think of the Stone Age as the time when humankind learned to make tools:

Peter **M**ade **N**ails.

OUR NEIGHBORS

Whether you live in a small state on the east coast or in a big Midwestern state, in a tiny Central American country or a giant Canadian province, you should know who your neighbors are—not just your next door neighbors on your street, but your neighbors nearby in the world. Here are clever ways to learn and remember their names.

These Great States

You know there are fifty states in the United States, and you can probably name a lot of them—but can you name them all? You'll be successful if you sing them. Try singing this song to the tune of the American folk song "Turkey in the Straw":

Alabama and Alaska, Arizona, Arkansas,
California, Colorado, Connecticut, and more.
Delaware, Florida, Georgia, Hawaii, Idaho,
Illinois, Indiana, Iowa . . . 35 to go . . .

Kansas and Kentucky, Louisiana, Maine,
Maryland, Massachusetts, and good old Michigan.
Minnesota, Mississippi, Missouri, and Montana,
Nebraska's 27, number 28's Nevada.

Next, New Hampshire and New Jersey, and way down, New Mexico.
There's New York, North Carolina, North Dakota, Ohio,
Oklahoma, Oregon, Pennsylvania, now let's see,
Rhode Island, South Carolina, South Dakota, Tennessee.

There's Texas and there's Utah, Vermont, I'm almost through,
Virginia and there's Washington, and West Virginia, too,
Could Wisconsin be the last state—is it just 49?
No, Wyoming is the last state in the 50 states that rhyme!

TOO COOL FOR SCHOOL
Several states have interesting shapes, but Michigan has the most memorable. It looks like a mitten. You can remember it as the high five state!

Fun Facts about States

Remembering facts about states is easier than remembering the names of all fifty states—you only have to remember a handful at a time!

There's one place in the United States where four states—**C**olorado, **A**rizona, **N**ew Mexico, and **U**tah—meet at one point. It's called the Four Corners. Here's an easy way to remember the states that touch:

I can remember the four states, **CAN U?**

Two states—**T**ennessee and **M**issouri—share the greatest number of borders (eight) with neighboring states. Remember them this way:

Touching **M**ost

The five largest states are easy to remember, starting with the biggest:

Alaska
Texas
California
Montana
New Mexico

Remember them this way:

Alison **T**ook **C**allie's **M**ath **N**otebook.

The five smallest states are easy to remember too. Here they are from smallest to largest:

Rhode Island
Delaware
Connecticut
New Jersey
New Hampshire

Just picture:

Rachel **D**rove **C**arefully **N**ear **N**eighbors.

Central American Countries

Central America consists of seven countries, plus part of Mexico. Here are the countries of Central America (including parts of Mexico), from northwest to southeast:

Mexico
Belize
Guatemala
El Salvador
Honduras
Nicaragua
Costa Rica
Panama

You'll never forget them if you picture this acrostic sentence:

My **B**ig **G**erbil **E**ats **H**is **N**ew **C**arrots **P**olitely.

Canadian Territories and Provinces

Just as you now know your neighbors to the south, you need to know your neighbors to the north. Canada has three territories and ten provinces. The territories are:

Northwest Territories

Nunavut

Yukon

The first three letters spell out **NNY**, or **N**ot **N**ew **Y**ork.

The Canadian provinces are:

British Columbia

Manitoba

Alberta

Ontario

Prince Edward Island

New Brunswick

Newfoundland and Labrador

Quebec

Nova Scotia

Saskatawan

You'll never forget the names of the provinces if you imagine this scene:

Baboons, **M**onkeys, **A**nd **O**rangutans **P**lay **N**oisy **N**intendo—"**Q**uiet," **N**ana **S**creams!

THE WORLD AROUND US

Take a look around your world and you'll see some amazing plants and animals—but you won't be able to see the atoms that make up the plants and animals and everything else. Your science teacher will want you to remember facts about plants, animals, atoms, and even the water cycle—whether you can see them or not!

Organizing Living Things

Now that you know all about the geography and geology of our planet, you need to know—and remember—how all living things are arranged into seven levels, or ranks. Some of the names of the levels are familiar (like *class*) and some sound weird (like *phylum*). Here are the seven levels:

Kingdom

Phylum

Class

Order

Family

Genus

Species

You can remember them this way:

Kids **P**lay **C**ards **O**n **F**reaky **G**ame **S**hows.

Classes of Animals

No, the animals are not sitting in math class! Scientists have divided all the animals in the world into two basic categories: vertebrates and invertebrates. A vertebrate is an animal that has a spine. Dogs, horses, and you are all vertebrates. A worm doesn't have a backbone, so it is an invertebrate.

Then scientists break down the animal categories even further, into classes. The six main classes of animals are:

Invertebrates
Fish
Amphibians
Reptiles
Mammals
Birds

Remember them like this:

I FARM Badly.

Back to the Beginning: Atoms

Atoms make up everything you see, hear, and touch—everything in the entire universe! And each atom is made up of **P**rotons, **E**lectrons, and **N**eutrons (or **PEN**). You can remember even more about them if you sing this song, written by Kathleen Crawford (to the tune of the theme song from "The Addams Family"):

They're tiny and they're teeny,
Much smaller than a beany,
They never can be seeny,
The Atoms Family.

> *Chorus:*
> They are so small.
> (Snap, snap)
> They're round like a ball.
> (Snap, snap)

They make up the air.
They're everywhere.
Can't see them at all.
(Snap, snap)

Together they make gases,
And liquids like molasses,

And all the solid masses,
The Atoms Family.

>   *Chorus*
>
>   Neutrons can be found,
>
>   Where protons hang around;
>
>   Electrons they surround
>
>   The Atoms Family.

Chorus

The Water Cycle

Water follows a circular pattern on Earth. It rises from lakes and rivers and oceans and other bodies of water into the atmosphere through **E**vaporation; through **C**ondensation it forms tiny droplets in clouds; then rain and other kinds of **P**recipitation return the water to earth, when the whole process starts all over again. All you need to remember is **ECP** or:

Every **C**loud **P**ops.

READING AND WRITING

The interjection cries out, "Hark!
I need an exclamation mark!"

PARTS OF SPEECH

You need to know the parts of speech to put together a sentence. There are several ways to remember the eight parts of speech:

Nouns
Verbs
Adjectives
Adverbs
Pronouns
Prepositions
Conjunctions
Interjections

You can recite this poem, of unknown authorship, which also teaches you what each part of speech does:

Every name is called a **noun,**
As *field* and *fountain*, *street* and *town.*

In place of noun the **pronoun** stands,
As *he* and *she* can clap their hands.

The **adjective** describes a thing,
As *magic* wand and *bridal* ring.

The **verb** means action, something done—
To *read,* to *write,* to *jump,* to *run.*

How things are done, the **adverbs** tell,
As *quickly, slowly, badly, well.*

The **preposition** shows relation,
As *in* the street, or *at* the station.

Conjunctions join, in many ways,
Sentences, words, *or* phrase *and* phrase.

The **interjection** cries out, "Hark!
I need an exclamation mark!"

Through poetry we learn how each
Of these make up the parts of speech.

TOO COOL FOR SCHOOL
Here's a fun grammar fact: Adverbs can modify, or apply meaning to, adjectives, but an adjective cannot modify an adverb.

If you want to include articles as the ninth part of speech, try out this poem, originally written for schoolchildren in the mid-nineteenth century by David B. Tower and Benjamin F. Tweed. Today's version includes a helpful last stanza to sum up the poem:

A **noun**'s the name of anything;
As, *school* or *garden*, *hoop* or *swing*.

Adjectives tell the kind of noun;
As, *great*, *small*, *pretty*, *white*, or *brown*.

Three of these words we often see
Called **articles**—*a, an,* and *the*.

Instead of nouns, the **pronouns** stand;
John's head, *his* face, *my* arm, *your* hand.

Verbs tell of something being done;
As, *read, write, spell, sing, jump,* or *run*.

How things are done, the **adverbs** tell;
As, *slowly, quickly, ill,* or *well*.

They also tell us where and when;
As, *here,* and *there,* and *now,* and *then*.

A **preposition** stands before
A noun; as, *in,* or *through,* a door.

Conjunctions sentences unite;
As, kittens scratch *and* puppies bite.

The **interjection** shows surprise;
As, *Oh! How pretty! Ah! How wise!*

The whole are called nine parts of speech,
Which reading, writing, speaking teach.

But maybe it's easier to remember a short phrase or sentence (as long as you understand what each part of speech does).

Pronoun
Adjective
Preposition
Adverb
Verb
Interjection
Noun
Conjunction
Article

You can think of **PAPA VINCA,** or perhaps, in a different order:

Patty **A**nd **I**saac **A**re **V**ery **C**areful **P**iercing **A**ll **N**oses.

Trust us, it'll look cool.

PUNCTUATION

Punctuation can be fun! You can use these tiny marks to completely change the meaning and tone of a sentence: "*Let's eat, grandpa,*" versus "*Let's eat grandpa*" (which is much more threatening). Punctuation also can give you time to breathe: Adam and Andy and Samantha and Carol went to the beach for a day without sunscreen; they got very sunburned. Or it can tell you when something is very dangerous: Watch out for the bear! These little marks have lots of power.

Here are easy ways to remember the main purpose of each punctuation mark. Pay attention to how each punctuation mark is used, as well as to each explanation.

Apostrophe An apostrophe proves that Angela's glove belongs to Angela. It proves that the boys' gloves belong to the boys. It also shows when a letter isn't (is not) where it's (it is) supposed to be.

Colon A colon is followed by an explanation or a list: It helps you breathe, think about the sentence, and pause.

Comma This mark helps you separate items, people, and other things on a list, and it separates two clauses in a sentence.

Dash Use a dash to create a pause in a sentence—or to interrupt a sentence with extra—or very important—information.

Exclamation point This mark is exciting!

Hyphen Put a hyphen between two words to create a first-class new word.

Period Stop.

Question mark Did you want to ask a question?

Semicolon Use a semicolon to link independent clauses; avoid using "and" over and over again.

EXTRA CREDIT

Can you write a sentence that includes a hyphen and a dash?

SPELLING DEMONS

Spelling can be tough, but it's always important to spell words right. Think how hard it would be to read that sentence if you spelled the words wrong: Speling can be tuff, but its alweeys important to spel words rite. See?

You'll find that some words follow rules (like "i before e"), some words ignore the rules (like *weird*), and some words seem to have completely made-up spelling (like *bruise*). So sometimes it helps to have tricks to remember the right way to write them. Here are those tricks for the tricky words. Look for capital letters in bold for clues on how to correctly spell:

Accept/Except

Your teacher will **A**ccept **A**nything **EX**cept **EX**cuses.

Accidentally

The car a**CC**identa**LL**y ran over Be**CC**a and E**LL**a.

Address

Be certain to **ADD** the **ADD**ress when you mail a letter.

Affect/Effect

Affect generally indicates **A**ction. (Being bad in class will **affect** my grade.) **E**ffect is the r**E**sult or **E**nd. (Studying hard had a good **effect** on my grade.)

Alien
A**LIE**ns **LIE** about outer space.

A lot
You'll need **A LOT** of money to buy **A LOT** on a lake.

Argument
I lost an **E** in an argument with my best friend.

Arithmetic
A Rat **I**n **T**he **H**ouse **M**ay **E**at **T**ony's **I**ce **C**ream.

Attendance
Your atten**DANCE** is required at the school **DANCE**.

Autumn
You need a **MN**emonic to remember autu**MN.**

Balloon
My **BALL**oon is round like a **BALL.**

Beautiful

Bald **E**agles **A**re **U**sually **BEAU**tiful.

Because

Big **E**lephants **C**an't **A**lways **U**se **S**mall **E**xits **BECAUSE** they're too big.

Believe

Never be**LIE**ve a **LIE.**

Break/Brake

If you br**EAK** that pot it will l**EAK**. T**AKE** your foot off the br**AKE**.

Breakfast

BREAK the window **FAST** before we get caught stealing **BREAKFAST.**

Bruise

A b**RUI**se can **RUI**n a f**RUI**t.

Burglar

A **LAR**ge burg**LAR** broke into my house.

Calendar

It gets **DAR**k toward the end of the calen**DAR** year.

Capital/Capitol

Capit**O**l has only **O**ne meaning: g**O**vernment buildings where people make laws. **AL**l the other meanings belong to capit**AL** (like capit**AL** letters and capit**AL** cities).

Cemetery

Rachel screamed "**E-E-E**" as she ran past the c**E**m**E**t**E**ry.

Chord/cord

A c**H**ord plays notes together in **H**armony. You have a spinal cord, vocal cords, and when you were born you had an umbilical cord—and none of them have an **H**.

Could (and would and should)

O U Lucky **D**uck, do you think you c**OULD** win the lottery?

Dear/Deer

Start each thank you note to **E**very **A**unt who gave you a present with "D**EA**r." A d**EE**r will look at you with its **EE**rie **E**y**E**s.

Colonel

The co**LONEL** standing guard was **LONEL**y.

Decision
CIndy and **SI**mon made a de**CISI**on together.

Definite
IT is positively defin**IT**e.

Desert/Dessert
A de**S**ert is **S**andy (one **S**), but de**SS**erts are **S**uper **S**weet (two **S**'s).

Disguise
Our **GUI**de through the haunted house was in dis**GUI**se.

Doubt
You might **B** wondering how to spell dou**B**t.

Eight
Ellen **I**magines **G**irls **H**ate **T**oads.

Embarrassed
I turn **R**eally **R**ed and **S**ilently **S**hake when I'm emba**R-R**a**SS**ed.

Excellent
I had an **EXC**ellent **EXC**use for not turning in my paper on time.

Exercise
EXERting yourself **C**an be w**ISE** in **EXERCISE.**

Familiar

The **LIAR** was fami**LIAR** with the questions on the quiz.

Fascinated

My **SCI**ence teacher is fa**SCI**nated by bugs.

February

BR! It's cold in Fe**BR**uary.

Forty

U are nowhere near forty years old!

Friend

A fri**END** is a friend until the **END** of time.

Giant

Don't **GI**ve **ANT**s **GIANT** food.

Government
A **GOVERN**ment has a job to do: **GOVERN.**

Grammar
My Grand**MA** thinks I have bad gram**MA**r.

Guarantee
Your **GUAR**antee **GUAR**ds your new MP3 player, even if it breaks.

Handsome
HAND SOME candy to that **HANDSOME** boy.

Hawaii
I like going watersk**ii**ng in Hawa**ii**.

Hear/Here
You h**EAR** with your **EAR**. W**HERE** are you? **HERE.**

Heroes
Her**OES** have the same number of t**OES** as everybody else.

Impossible
Some **S**ay the B**IBLE** stories are impo**SSIBLE**.

Instead
My mother always asks for coffee ins**TEA**d of **TEA.**

Independent

The indepen**DENT** kid put a **DENT** in his bicycle.

Interrupt
It is **R**eally **R**ude to inte**RR**upt someone when they're speaking.

Island
What is an **ISLAND?** It **IS LAND** surrounded by water.

Juice
U and **I** like j**UI**ce.

Kindergarten
I think **ART** is one of the best parts of kinderg**ART**en.

Knew/New
He **K**ept working until he **K**new his times tables; when he finished, there was **N**othing **N**ew for him to learn.

Library
Your **BRA**in gets a workout at the li**BRA**ry.

License
I'd **LI**ke this **CEN**tury to **SE**e my driver's **LICENSE**.

Lightning
There's no **E** in light, and there's no **E** in lightning.

Lose/Loose
L**O**se lost an **O**; l**OO**ps are l**OO**se.

Marriage

You and **I** are in this marr**I**age together.

Minute

Yo**U** would never expect to find a **U** in min**U**te.

Mississippi

MISS IS SIPPIng her iced tea in **MISSISSIPPI.**

Misspell

If you mi**SS** the **S**econd **S,** you will mi**SS**pell a tricky word.

Necessary

You have **one C**ollar on your shirt, but you wear **two S**ocks; all are ne**C**e**SS**ary when you get dressed.

Neighbor

Our new n**EIGH**bor **E**d **I**s **G**enuinely **H**appy he moved.

Niece

My **NI**e**CE** is a **NICE** person.

Occasion

Choose a **C**ard for her **S**pecial o**CC**a**S**ion.

Ocean

Only **C**lowns **E**at **A**t **N**ight by the **OCEAN**.

Nineteen

NINE TEENs ate **NINETEEN** pizzas and then threw up.

Often

One out **OF TEN** baseball players **OFTEN** strike out.

Orchestra

The **ORCH**estra played on the p**ORCH**.

Parallel

Not a**LL L**ines you see are Para**LL**e**L.**

People

Peter **E**ats **O**ften; **P**eter **L**ikes **E**ating.

Permanent

The braid in the horse's **MANE** was not per**MANE**nt.

Pleasant

PLainly, **EA**ting **S**alty **ANT**s is not **PLEASANT.**

Principal/Principle

A princi**PAL** is your **PAL;** princi**LE**s are ru**LE**s.

Quiet

U and **I E**at q**UIE**tly.

Question

QUick! **E**xplain **S**omething **T**o **I**van—**O**r **N**ot.

Recognize

How does a d**OG** rec**OG**nize his friends?

Receive

R-E-C-E Is a **V**ery **E**asy way to remember how to spell **RECEIVE.**

Relief

My teacher needed to **LIE** down to get re**LIE**f from her badly behaved class.

Restaurant

L**AURA** worked at the new rest**AURA**nt.

Rhyme

Really **H**appy? **Y**ou **M**ight **E**xplode!

Rhythm

Rhythm **H**elps **Y**our **T**wo **H**ips **M**ove.

Scissors

S**C**i**SS**ors **C**ut **S**uch **S**harp pieces of paper!

Separate

I smell a **RAT** in sepa**RAT**e.

Sincerely

You can always **RELY** on me, since**RELY.**

Stationery/Stationary

P**E**ns, pap**E**r, and **E**nvelopes are pieces of station**E**ry.
A p**AR**ked c**AR** is station**AR**y.

Surprise

R you surprised by the **R** in su**R**prise?

Sword

Playing with a **SW**ord is **SW**ell.

Temperature

Ellen's **E**xtremely m**ATURE** when I take her t**E**mp**E**r**ATURE**.

Tomorrow

TOM will be **R**eady to **R**ace **TOM**o**RR**ow.

Tongue

TONs of G**LUE** taste terrible on your **TONGUE.**

Vacuum

Can **U** **U**nderstand why we have to va**CUU**m?

Vegetable

Evan **E**ats **TABLE**s full of v**E**g**ETABLE**s.

Vitamin

Vita**MIN**s never taste as good as **MIN**ts.

Wednesday

Alex **WED** Va**NES**sa to**DAY** (**WEDNESDAY**).

Weird

WE are considered **WE**ird.

Your/You're

OUR home is y**OUR** home. **YOU'RE** always welcome here, **YOU** a**RE**!

THE MYSTERIES
OF HISTORY

*In fourteen hundred ninety-two,
Columbus sailed the ocean blue...*

IT'S ANCIENT HISTORY

Greek philosophers, Roman emperors, and the seven wonders of the ancient world seem like ancient history because . . . well, they *are* ancient history! But they're still important to know, so here's what you need to remember.

Greek Philosophers

Some of the first stories about people and places came from ancient Greece. And many of these stories are told by or about the great thinkers, or philosophers, named:

Socrates (469–399 BC)

Plato (c.428–c.348 BC)

Aristotle (384–322 BC)

Socrates taught Plato, and Plato taught Aristotle, and together they taught people ways to think and act. Together their names spell **SPA;** you can remember that they gave **S**uper **P**opular **A**dvice.

Roman Emperors

Maybe you've heard of Julius Caesar, the Roman dictator who was assassinated in 44 BC, but have you heard of the emperors who came after him?

Augustus (27 BC–AD 14)

Tiberius (AD 14–37)

Caligula (AD 37–41)

Claudius (AD 41–54)

Nero (AD 54–68)

Though these emperors didn't give Super Popular Advice (they were often tough and greedy rulers), you can remember them this way:

All **T**ried **C**ounting **C**oins **N**ightly.

Seven Wonders of the Ancient World

Though it's fun to think that something you've built is one of the wonders of the world, the real seven wonders of the ancient world are:

Statue of Zeus at Olympia

Lighthouse of Alexandria

Mausoleum of Halicarnassus

Pyramids of Egypt

Hanging Gardens of Babylon

Temple of Artemis at Ephesus

Colossus of Rhodes

Think about a girl named Martha taking a test about the seven wonders of the world:

Seems **L**ike **M**artha **P**assed **H**er **T**est **C**almly.

EXTRA CREDIT

Can you come up with an acrostic sentence for the seven wonders of the world using S, L, M, P, H, T, C?

Can you think of an acrostic sentence using the same letters, but in reverse order (C, T, H, P, M, L, S)?

AMERICAN HISTORY

From the discovery of the new world to the most recent president of the United States, American history is filled with colorful characters, dramatic moments, and world-changing events. Learning about these people, places, and adventures is great fun, but it can be difficult too: Can you name the original thirteen colonies? When exactly did the Civil War start? How many presidents have been assassinated while in office—and who were they? The answers are all here, as well as the tricks you need to remember them.

Christopher Columbus

Every schoolchild has heard about Christopher Columbus and the discovery of America, and probably remembers the date this way:

> In fourteen hundred ninety-two,
> Columbus sailed the ocean blue.

These are the first two lines of a poem called "The History of the U.S." by Winifred Sackville Stoner, Jr. The whole first stanza includes two more lines:

> In fourteen hundred ninety-two,
> Columbus sailed the ocean blue
> And found this land, land of the Free,
> Beloved by you, beloved by me.

The last two lines round out the first stanza nicely, but don't really help you remember anything. Stick with the first two lines.

The Pilgrims

Winifred Stoner's poem also can help you remember when Jamestown was founded, and when the pilgrims landed on Plymouth Rock.

And in the year sixteen and seven,
Good Captain Smith thought he'd reach Heav'n,
And then he founded Jamestown City,
Alas, 'tis gone, oh, what a pity . . .

In sixteen twenty, pilgrims saw
Our land that had no unjust law.
Their children live here to this day
Proud citizens of USA.

The Thirteen Colonies

Maybe your state is one of the original thirteen colonies, or maybe it's not. Either way, you'll probably have to memorize them for school. Thirteen is a lot to remember, no matter what mnemonic device you use. But if you break the colonies down by region, you'll have fewer to remember at a time. Put them all together, and you'll be sure to impress your teacher!

New England Colonies:

New Hampshire

Massachusetts

Rhode Island

Connecticut

Just remember:

No **M**ore **R**aw **C**arrots!

Middle Colonies:

New York

New Jersey

Delaware

Pennsylvania

Now try this:

Now **N**o **D**ried **P**runes!

Southern Colonies:

> **M**aryland
> **S**outh Carolina
> **V**irginia
> **G**eorgia
> **N**orth Carolina

Just think:

> **M**aybe **S**ome **V**ery **G**ood **N**uts.

Put them all together, and they become even more memorable:

> **N**o **M**ore **R**aw **C**arrots! **N**ow **N**o **D**ried **P**runes! **M**aybe **S**ome **V**ery **G**ood **N**uts.

The Civil War

You have to remember a lot of facts about wars—the causes of the war, the important battles, and dates of important events that occurred during the war. Here's a poem that will help you remember important Civil War dates: the start of the war (1861), the date the Emancipation Proclamation was issued (1863), and the end of the war (1865):

In 1861 the war had begun.

In 1862 the bullets still flew.

In 1863 Lincoln set slaves free.

In 1864 there still was war.

In 1865 hardly a man is alive.

When you study the Civil War, you learn about the Union and the Confederacy, and which states fall into each category. You may also need to know the order in which the Confederate states seceded from the Union:

South Carolina

Mississippi

Florida

Alabama

Georgia

Louisiana

Texas

Virginia

Arkansas

North Carolina

Tennessee

You probably won't forget the order of these states if you imagine your friend doing something this crazy:

So **M**y **F**riend **A**te **G**iant **L**izards **T**uesday; **V**omited **A**ll **N**ight **T**uesday.

EXTRA CREDIT
You know that there were eleven Confederate states during the Civil War. How many states formed the Union?

The Presidents

The United States has had forty-four presidents. If you can remember forty-four names, you should win a prize! Maybe you can remember them in smaller groups. Group number one includes the first seven presidents (and the years they served as president). These are the early presidents you'll hear most about in school.

George **W**ashington (1789–1797)

John **A**dams (1797–1801)

Thomas **J**efferson (1801–1809)

James **M**adison (1809–1817)

James **M**onroe (1817–1825)

John Quincy **A**dams (1825–1829)

Andrew **J**ackson (1829–1837)

Think of the presidents chatting with one of your relatives:

Washington **A**nd **J**efferson **M**et **M**y **A**unt **J**enny.

With the exception of Abraham Lincoln and Ulysses S. Grant, you probably won't have to know a lot about the middle presidents—including the order in which they served—but you should at least be familiar with their names:

Martin **V**an Buren (1837–1841)

William Henry **H**arrison (1841)

John **T**yler (1841–1845)

James **P**olk (1845–1849)

Zachary **T**aylor (1849–1850)

Millard **F**illmore (1850–1853)

Franklin **P**ierce (1853–1857)

James **B**uchanan (1857–1861)

Abraham **L**incoln (1861–1865)

Andrew **J**ohnson (1865–1869)

Ulysses S. **G**rant (1869–1877)

Rutherford B. **H**ayes (1877–1881)

James **G**arfield (1881)

Chester **A**rthur (1881–1885)

Grover **C**leveland (1885–1889)

Benjamin **H**arrison (1889–1893)

Grover **C**leveland (1893–1897)

William **M**cKinley (1897–1901)

If you have to remember their names, try splitting the list of presidents into four almost equal pieces, and picture boys playing sports:

Vinnie **H**ates **T**o **P**lay **T**ennis.
(**V**an Buren, **H**arrison, **T**yler, **P**olk, **T**aylor)

Frank **P**lays **B**aseball **L**azily.
(**F**illmore, **P**ierce, **B**uchanan, **L**incoln)

Jim **G**oes **H**iking **G**ladly.
(**J**ohnson, **G**rant, **H**ayes, **G**arfield)

Andy **C**limbs **H**igh **C**loudy **M**ountains.
(**A**rthur, **C**leveland, **H**arrison, **C**leveland, **M**cKinley)

EXTRA CREDIT
Without looking at the list of presidents, can you remember how many presidents have been named George? John? James?

In order to memorize the most recent presidents, divide them into two groups: the early twentieth century presidents and the late twentieth century through early twenty-first century presidents.

The early twentieth century presidents are:

Theodore **R**oosevelt (1901–1909)
William H. **T**aft (1909–1913)
Woodrow **W**ilson (1913–1921)
Warren **H**arding (1921–1923)
Calvin **C**oolidge (1923–1929)
Herbert **H**oover (1929–1933)
Franklin D. **R**oosevelt (1933–1945)
Harry S. **T**ruman (1945–1953)

Even though this sentence has nothing to do with presidents, you'll probably remember it—and the presidents:

Really **T**all **W**omen **H**ate **C**urly **H**air, **R**ough **T**eeth.

The late twentieth century and early twenty-first century presidents are:

Dwight D. **E**isenhower (1953–1961)
John F. **K**ennedy (1961–1963)
Lyndon B. **J**ohnson (1963–1969)
Richard M. **N**ixon (1969–1974)
Gerald **F**ord (1974–1977)
Jimmy **C**arter (1977–1981)
Ronald **R**eagan (1981–1989)
George H. W. **B**ush (1989–1993)
William J. **C**linton (1993–2001)
George W. **B**ush (2001–2009)
Barack **O**bama (2009–)

Think of the presidents playing croquet with this sentence, and you'll be able to remember the recent presidents:

Even **K**en **J**oined **N**ancy **F**or **C**roquet; **R**ob **B**elieves **C**roquet's **B**asically **O**dd.

The Presidents Assassinated in Office

Your teacher may want you to know the order of the presidents, but your friends will be more impressed with a list of presidents who have been assassinated while in office:

Lincoln
Garfield
McKinley
Kennedy

Since all four were shot, remember their assassinations with this clever sentence:

Lunatic **G**unmen **M**ight **K**ill.

Mount Rushmore

The giant heads of four US presidents—**W**ashington, **J**efferson, **R**oosevelt, and **L**incoln—are carved into the face of Mount Rushmore in South Dakota. Each head is sixty feet high! Here's an easy way to remember which presidents appear at Mount Rushmore and the order they appear in, from left to right:

We **J**udge **R**ushmore **L**ikeable.

> **TOO COOL FOR SCHOOL**
> *Washington's nose is twenty-one feet long on Mount Rushmore. The other noses are twenty feet long.*

The Wright Brothers

Everybody learns about Orville and Wilbur Wright and how they made the first successful airplane flight. Do you remember when? Use this rhyme to jog your memory:

The Wright Brothers flew free in 1903.

BRITISH HISTORY

Kings and queens are the rock stars of England, even those who have been dead a long, long time. Sometimes they're best known for their bad behavior, like Henry VIII, who caused the deaths of several of his six wives. Impress your friends and family by remembering details about these fascinating people.

Kings and Queens

England has been ruled by more than forty kings and queens—way too many to remember, whether you recited a poem with their names or a very long acrostic sentence using their initials. Instead, you might want to remember the names of the main royal families—or dynastic houses—that have ruled England for centuries.

Norman

Plantagenet

Lancaster

York

Tudor

Stuart

Hanover

Windsor

Think about opening your history book and reciting this sentence:

Nervous **P**eople **L**ike **Y**ou **T**ry **S**tudying **H**istory **W**eekly.

Henry VIII

King Henry VIII of England (1491–1547) is remembered for many things, but he's probably remembered best for having six wives. His wives are remembered for what happened to them.

Henry's wives, in order of when he married them, are:

Catherine of Aragon
Anne Boleyn
Jane Seymour
Anne of Cleves
Catherine Howard
Catherine Parr

If you keep in mind that Kate is a nickname for Catherine, you can remember Henry VIII's wives this way:

Kate and Anne and Jane and Anne and Kate again and again!

And what happened to each of them? The following rhyme tells you all you need to know about the fate of each wife (in order of the wives):

Divorced, beheaded, died,
Divorced, beheaded, survived.

MAGICAL MATH

Numerator goes Up,
Denominator goes Down.

ALL ABOUT NUMBERS

Even if you're not in love with math class (and especially if you are!), you have to admit that numbers can be kind of cool. They let you count money, dial a phone, and measure the distance between your house and your friend's house. And sometimes they act like a secret code: What number is Super Bowl XLVI anyway? Unlock the code, and you'll unlock a whole new world!

Roman Numerals

Way back in ancient Rome, people used letters in place of numbers. The Romans were nice enough to skip a Roman numeral for zero—giving you one less Roman numeral to remember—but they did have seven numbers that you'll see on occasion.

I = 1
V = 5
X = 10
L = 50
C = 100
D = 500
M = 1,000

Try remembering them this way:

I Viewed **X**-rays; **L**acrosse **C**aused **D**amaged **M**uscles.

If you can remember **IVX** (the first three Roman numerals) without a sentence, you can remember the rest with these phrases:

Lucy **C**ries **D**uring **M**ovies.

Lonely **C**ows **D**on't **M**oo.

The Metric System

You're probably not too familiar with the metric system, and your parents may not be either. Still, you need to remember the names of metric measurements for school (because you'll run into them in science). The metric measurements for distance use a meter as a starting point.

Kilometer = 1,000 meters

Hectometer = 100 meters

Decameter = 10 meters

Meter = 1 meter

Decimeter = 1/10 of a meter

Centimeter = 1/100 of a meter

Millimeter = 1/1,000 of a meter

The easiest way to remember these seven numbers is to use their first letters in a silly sentence:

King **H**enry **D**ied **M**errily **D**rinking **C**hocolate **M**ilk.

Now that you can remember the order of distance in the metric system, you can conquer the order of weight in the metric system. Just use the same prefixes (kilo-, hecto-, deca-, deci-, centi-, and milli-), but substitute *gram* for *meter*. Your new, sadder sentence will look like this:

King **H**enry **D**ied **G**rimly **D**rinking **C**hocolate **M**ilk.

EXTRA CREDIT
Can you come up with a sentence for the order of metric weights that starts with **kangaroo?**

Prime Numbers

A prime number is a number that can be divided by itself and by 1—that's all. So 2, 3, 5, 7, 11, 13, and 17 are all prime numbers. How can you remember what makes a prime number a prime number?

If I'm a prime number, I only think of the **me** in pri**me**. Turn the **i** in pr**i**me to a 1, and you'll never forget that a prime number can only be divided by me (itself) and 1.

Fractions

A fraction—a number that is not a whole number, like 2/5—is divided into two parts: a numerator and a denominator. The numerator is the top number (in this case, the number 2) and the denominator is the bottom number (in this case, the number 5). How to keep them straight?

N**U**merator goes **U**p, **D**enominator goes **D**own.

Or you can use two words that go together to let you know that the **N** comes before the **D** in a fraction:

Nice **D**og
North **D**akota

MULTIPLYING AND DIVIDING

Even if adding and subtracting are easy for you, multiplying and dividing can be a little more challenging. But you can learn tricks—including an amazing trick with your hands—that will help you become a multiplying and dividing whiz.

Tricks for Times Tables

The best way to learn your times tables is to memorize them. You can make up rhymes to help you remember times tables—or parts of them—that give you trouble, but learning mnemonics for all the times tables would be harder than learning the times tables alone!

However, there are tricks that can help you remember two complete times tables. The first is for the ten times table: Want to multiply a number by ten? Just add a zero to the original number and you have your answer.

$$4 \times 10 = 40$$
$$16 \times 10 = 160$$

Be sure to move the comma to the right by one place when you start multiplying larger numbers by 10:

$$2,789 \times 10 = 27,890$$

The nine times table has an even better trick. Look carefully at the product (the answer) of the nine times tables up to 10:

$$9 \times 1 = 9$$
$$9 \times 2 = 18$$
$$9 \times 3 = 27$$
$$9 \times 4 = 36$$

$9 \times 5 = 45$
$9 \times 6 = 54$
$9 \times 7 = 63$
$9 \times 8 = 72$
$9 \times 9 = 81$
$9 \times 10 = 90$

Do you see a pattern? Here's the secret. Add the digits in the product together, and they will always equal 9.

$9 \times 4 = 36 \ (3 + 6 = 9)$
$9 \times 8 = 72 \ (7 + 2 = 9)$

Seems obvious now, right?

Here's an even easier way to learn your nine times tables—just look at your hands. What's the trick?

Hold your hands up, with your palms facing you. Starting with the thumb on your left hand, give each thumb and finger a number. Your left thumb is one, your next finger in line is two, then three, and so on, until you reach your right thumb, which will be the number ten.

Now try 9×2. Bend your left index finger (the one you labeled number two) down to your palm (or as close as you can get) to represent the two in 9×2. Now count the number of fingers (and thumbs) standing to the left of your index finger, and you have one (thumb). Count the number of fingers (and thumbs) standing to the right of your index finger—eight. Put them next to each other and you have 18—the product of 9×2!

Try it with 9×4. Bend your left ring finger (the one you labeled number four) down to your palm. How many fingers and thumbs do you have to the left of your ring finger? Three. How many fingers and thumbs do you have to the right of your ring finger? Six. Put them next to each other for 36—the product of 9 x 4.

You can use this trick all the way to 9 x 10. If you bend your right thumb down, you have nine fingers and thumbs to the left, and zero fingers and thumbs to the right. Together they make 90!

Remember that the number to the left side of the bent finger belongs in the tens column of the answer, and the number to the right side of the bent finger belongs in the ones column.

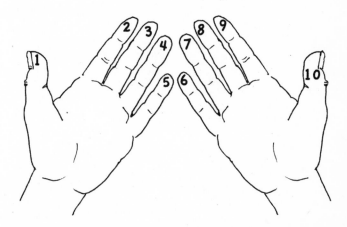

Long Division

Long division requires certain steps, just as a dance requires certain steps. In long division, though, the steps are not nearly as fancy as dance steps.

Divide
Multiply
Subtract
Bring down

The easiest way to remember the order of the steps is the mnemonic they probably teach you in school:

Dad, **M**om, **S**ister, **B**rother.

If you need to see a picture in your head to remember the steps, try:

Dumb **M**onkeys **S**teal **B**ananas.

If you want to add the word *down* in the final step (*bring down*), try remembering the steps this way:

Dracula's **M**other **S**ucks **B**lood **D**aily

CALCULATE THIS!

Here's where you take what you've learned about numbers to a whole new level. You can figure out the toughest problems if you know the correct order of operations, and you'll easily figure out the mode, median, and mean of a set of numbers with the mnemonic devices below.

Order of Operations

Math problems start getting complicated once you've mastered the basics of adding, subtracting, multiplying, and dividing. Now you need to add, subtract, multiply, and divide all in one problem! Throw in an exponent, and you have your work cut out for you. Sometimes you'll see a problem like this:

$$(8-3) \times 2^2 + 6 \div 3 = X$$

. . . and you have to figure out what **X** is. You must do each operation in a particular order or you'll get the wrong answer. What's the correct order?

Parentheses

Exponents

Multiplication

Division

Addition

Subtraction

Pretty much everybody remembers the order of operations with this sentence:

Please **E**xcuse **M**y **D**ear **A**unt **S**ally.

If you need to see an image to help you remember the right order, try this:

Pandas **E**at **M**y **D**oughnuts **A**fter **S**chool.

And by the way, the answer is 22. Did you get it right?

Averages

Finding an average isn't as easy as just finding an average. There are three main ways to do it, and you need to remember which way is the right way when solving a math problem. You have to remember mode, median, and mean.

Here's how:

Mode This is the number that appears most often in a set of numbers. For example, if you have this set of numbers—1, 2, 2, 8, 9, 11, 16—the mode number is 2.

The **MO**de number appears **MO**st often.

Median This is the number that you'll find exactly in the middle of a set of numbers that are listed in order. In that same set of numbers—1, 2, 2, 8, 9, 11, 16—the median number is 8.

The me**D**ian number is the mi**D**dle number.

(If you have a set of numbers that doesn't have only one middle number—say 1, 2, 2, 8, 9, 11—you'll add the two middle numbers together and then divide the total by two: 2 + 8 = 10 ÷ 2 = 5.)

Mean This is what you get when you add all the numbers in the set together, then divide that sum by how many numbers are in the set. Let's use the same set again: add 1, 2, 2, 8, 9, 11, and 16 for a total of 49. Divide 49 by 7 (how many numbers appear in the set), and you have a mean of 7. You can also call this the average.

Remember: Someone **mean** might call you **average.**

GEOMETRY

You need to master the difference between parallel and perpendicular lines if you're studying geometry, and then you need to learn the ins and outs of angles, triangles, and circles. Here are fun and clever ways to remember what you need to know.

Parallel and Perpendicular

What are parallel lines? Lines that never meet each other or grow farther apart from each other, even if they go on forever. Picture the two l's in para**LL**el as parallel lines.

para**LL**el

What are perpendicular lines? Lines that come together to form a ninety degree angle. The **e**'s in P**E**rp**E**ndicular are examples of perpendicular lines; the horizontal lines are perpendicular to the vertical line of the capital letter **E**.

p**E**rp**E**ndicular

Angles

When you start learning about geometry, you start learning about angles.

Right angles are ninety degree angles.

Remember them this way:

Sit **RIGHT** up so your body forms a ninety degree angle.

Acute angles are angles that are less than ninety degrees.

Just think:

An **ACUTE** angle is **A CUTE** angle because it's so small.

Obtuse angles are angles between ninety and 180 degrees.

Picture this:

OBtuse angles are the biggest, fattest angles—they're **OB**ese.

You also need to know—and remember—the difference between complementary angles and supplementary angles. Two angles are complementary if they add up to ninety degrees, while two angles are supplementary if they add up to 180 degrees.

Complementary angles start with the letter **C,** which comes before the letter **S** (for supplementary) in the alphabet.

And . . . complementary angles (adding up to ninety degrees) come before supplementary angles (adding up to 180 degrees) in terms of size.

So . . . complementary angles are smaller. Supplementary angles are bigger.

If you want to remember the angles by putting an image in your head, remember that **C**omplementary angles form **C**ool **C**orners.

Triangles

As you learn more about geometry and angles, you'll learn more about triangles. You can have a right triangle (with one right—or ninety degree—angle), an acute triangle (where all angles are less than ninety degrees), or an obtuse triangle (which has an angle greater than ninety degrees). There are three other kinds of triangles too: equilateral, isosceles, and scalene.

All three sides of an **EQU**ilateral triangle are the same length, or **EQU**al. All three angles are equal too.

An isosceles triangle has two sides that are the same length and two angles that are the same size. It looks like a Christmas tree. Sing this song (to the tune of "O, Christmas Tree") to help you remember its shape:

> Oh, isosceles, oh isosceles,
> Two angles have
> Equal degrees.
> Oh, isosceles, oh, isosceles,
> You look just like
> A Christmas tree.

TOO COOL FOR SCHOOL
You can sometimes take the names of two triangles and combine them to form a new type of triangle. For example, a right isosceles triangle has a right angle (ninety degrees) and two equal sides.

Equilateral   Isosceles   Scalene

A scalene triangle has a mind of its own. Every side is a different length, and every angle is different too. Remember what a scalene triangle looks like by remembering what it's not:

Scale**NE** means the sides and angles are **N**ot **E**qual.

If you want to remember the triangles by how they look compared to each other, keep this in mind:

Equilateral triangles have three equal sides and three equal angles.

Isosceles triangles have two equal sides and two equal angles.

Scalene triangles have no equal sides and no equal angles.

Remember them in that order by thinking:

Everyone **I**s **S**omeone.

Even **I**guanas **S**leep.

Circles

You know what a circle looks like, but did you know that it's defined as a shape with all points the same distance from the center? There are a few other things you need to know about circles. Here's how to remember them:

Circumference The distance around the edge of a circle is called the circumference. (The distance around the edge of any other two-dimensional shape is called the perimeter.)

Just think:

CIRCumference is the distance around a **CIRC**le.

Diameter The distance across the circle (through the center) is the diameter.

Remember:

Measure the **DI**ameter **DI**rectly across the circle.

TOO COOL FOR SCHOOL

You see lots of symbols when you're studying math, including > and <. These two symbols mean greater than (>) and less than (<). If you want to say that 10 is greater than 7, you'd write 10 > 7. If you want to say that 3 is less than 9, you'd write 3 < 9. Think of the open part of the symbol as the open mouth of an alligator; he has to open his mouth really wide for the larger number, and not so wide for the smaller number. See how the open part always faces the larger number?

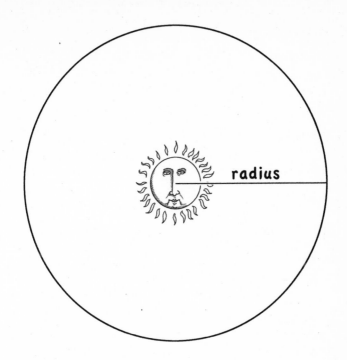

Radius The distance from the center of the circle to any point on the edge of the circle is the radius. Imagine that the center of the circle is the sun, and rays of sunshine are shooting out from the sun.

Picture it like this:

One **RA**y of sunshine forms the **RA**dius of a circle.

If you take one radius and attach it end-to-end to another radius so that it forms a straight line, you'll have exactly one diameter.

Keep this in mind:

Double the radius to get the **D**iameter.

THE SOUNDS
OF MUSIC

Empty Garbage Before Dad Flips.

THE NOTES

Learning how to read music is like learning how to read a code. And breaking this code is really rewarding because when you do it right, you end up making beautiful music!

You know your ABCs inside and out, so applying them to musical notes won't be hard. In fact, you'll use only the first seven letters of the alphabet in music notation. Each note in music uses one of these seven letters. These letters in a row make a musical scale. If you can remember A, B, C, D, E, F, and G, you can remember one very important part of reading music. The hard part comes with figuring out the order the letters belong in, which depends on what you see in your music book.

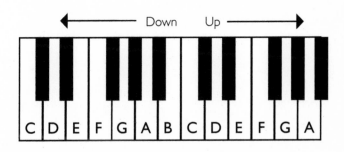

Most scales are made up of eight notes, and each scale usually starts and ends with the same letter. The last note is eight notes higher (or lower) than the first one in the scale. The scale of C major, for example, starts with C and ends with C and looks like this: C, D, E, F, G, A, B, C. The distance from the first C to the second C is called an octave, and the two Cs plus the six letters between them make up the eight letters in a one octave scale.

Remember:

A one **oct**ave scale has eight notes. An **oct**agon has eight sides. An **oct**opus has eight legs.

TOO COOL FOR SCHOOL

A flute generally has a range of three octaves. A cello has a range of four octaves, and a piano has a range of 7¹ü₃ octaves.

THE STAFF

A staff is a set of five parallel lines and four spaces. Musicians write their music on the staff. Each line and each space represents one of the seven letters. At the beginning of each staff you'll see a symbol called a clef—either a 𝄢, meaning bass clef, or 𝄞, meaning treble clef. The bass clef tells you that you need to play the lower notes; on the piano, you generally play these notes with your left hand. The treble clef tells you that you need to play the higher notes, and on the piano you usually play these notes with your right hand.

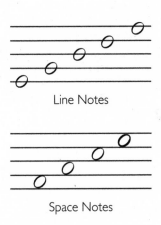

Line Notes

Space Notes

Bass Clef Lines

The notes on the lines of the bass clef follow a particular order; going from the bottom line to the top line, they are: **G, B, D, F, A.** The best way to remember the order of the notes is to think of a sentence that will stick in your mind (see page 132).

Good **B**agels **D**on't **F**all **A**part.

Great **B**ig **D**ogs **F**ight **A**nimals.

Great **B**ig **D**ucks **F**ly **A**way.

Bass Clef Spaces

From bottom to top, the notes in the spaces in the bass clef are **A, C, E,** and **G**. The classic way to remember the spaces is:

All **C**ows **E**at **G**rass.

If you want to be a little more creative, you can remember:

All **C**hildren **E**arn **G**rades.

Amazing **C**lowns **E**ntertain **G**irls.

… But since the simplest is often the easiest to remember, you might want to stick with the chewing cows.

Treble Clef Lines

The notes on the lines of the treble clef are **E, G, B, D, F,** from the bottom line to the top line. You can remember these notes with the common sayings:

Every **G**ood **B**oy **D**eserves **F**udge (or **F**un or **F**avors).

Every **G**ood **B**oy **D**oes **F**ine.

...But sometimes it's more fun to have a silly image in your head:

Empty **G**arbage **B**efore **D**ad **F**lips.

Treble Clef Spaces

The treble clef spaces may be the last you learn, but they're certainly the easiest:

FACE

The bottom space is **F** and the top space is **E.** There's no need for a rhyme or a funny sentence here. Just spell **FACE.**

> **TOO COOL FOR SCHOOL**
> The treble clef started out looking like the letter G because the treble clef represented the G above middle C. It evolved over time into the symbol used today.

SHARPS AND FLATS

You probably know that the scale of C major is the easiest to play because it doesn't have any sharps or flats. A sharp note is half a step higher than a natural (all white) note—the A, B, C, D, E, F, G notes you learned at the beginning of this chapter. This means that the sharp is the closest black or white note up from each white note.

Remember sharps like this:

If you sit on something **sharp,** you jump **UP.**

A flat note is half a step lower than a natural (all white) note. This means that the flat is the closest black or white note down from each white note.

Picture this:

If a chair is **flat,** you sit **DOWN** on it.

Flat tires go **DOWN.**

EXTRA CREDIT

Can you think of an acrostic sentence that will help you remember "Sharp is Up, Flat is Down"?

Different scales need different sharps and flats to make them sound right. The scale of D major needs two sharps (F$^\sharp$ and C$^\sharp$), while the scale of E$^\flat$ major needs three flats (B$^\flat$, E$^\flat$, and A$^\flat$). The sharps or flats listed next to the clef signs on the staff are called the key signature. The key signature tells you which letters to automatically change from natural to sharp or flat. So if you see the symbol for a flat on the line for a B, you will play all of the B notes as B♭.

The Order of Sharps

A shortcut to remembering the order of sharps in key signatures is to keep this order in mind:

F, C, G, D, A, E, B

If there is only one sharp, it will be F♯. If there are two sharps, they will be F♯ and C♯, and so on.

Try thinking of one of these sentences to help you remember the order of sharps:

Fred's **C**ousin **G**ets **D**izzy **A**fter **E**very **B**eer.

Fat **C**ows **G**raze **D**aily **A**t **E**d's **B**arn.

Frogs **C**an't **G**o **D**iving **A**fter **E**ating **B**reakfast.

The Order of Flats

Now you need to remember the order of flats in key signatures. Here is the order:

B, E, A, D, G, C, F

If there is only one flat, it is B$\flat$. If there are two flats, they are B$\flat$ and E$\flat$ and so on.

Try thinking of one of the following sentences to help you with the order of flats:

Bobby **E**ats **A D**og, **G**oat, **C**at, and **F**rog.

Billy **E**xplodes **A**nd **D**ad **G**ets **C**ompletely **F**reaked.

Did you notice that the order of flats is the order of sharps backward?

DYNAMICS

Whether you play the piano, the clarinet or the trumpet, you need to pay attention to the dynamics of the piece you're playing—the details that give the music life.

Tempo

Composers put comments in the music they write that tell you to play the music fast, slow, or somewhere in between. Unfortunately, their notes are in another language, so sometimes it's hard to remember what they're trying to say. Think of their instructions like this:

ViVace = **V**ery fast and li**V**ely

al**LEG**ro = fast (Use your **LEG**s to go fast.)

MODERato = **MODER**ate or medium

ANdante = slow (An **AN**chor will slow down your boat.)

adagio = very slow (Adagio means very slow.)

Volume

Along with tempo, composers want you to play their piece—or parts of their piece—loud, soft, or somewhere in between. They tell you what volume they prefer by marking their score with these words:

fortissimo = very loud

forte = loud

mezzo forte = medium loud

mezzo piano = medium soft

piano = soft

pianissimo = very soft

Since the terms are similar, learning a mnemonic for each individual term probably won't help you remember their meanings. But if you remember the range of the terms—from fortissimo to pianissimo, or very loud to very soft—you may have a better chance of remembering what each term means. Try imagining flying fish to remember the range of volume:

Flying **F**ish **M**ainly **M**imic **P**laying **P**iano.

TOO COOL FOR SCHOOL

*Some composers use extreme dynamics in their pieces. Few pieces contain more than three ƒs—ƒ stands for forte (loud), **ƒƒ** stands for fortissimo (very loud), and **ƒƒƒ** stands for fortississimo (extremely loud)—but the Russian composer P. I. Tchaikovsky uses **ƒƒƒƒ** in passages in his 1812 Overture.*

Staccato and Legato

Your music teacher or the composer of your piece may tell you to play a particular note or notes staccato or legato. What does this mean?

If you play a **ST**accato note, you play a short, crisp note; you **ST**ab at the note.

If you play several notes leg**AT**o, you play them smoothly and connected; you link them **A**ll **T**ogether.

> ### EXTRA CREDIT
> *Along with staccato notes, you can have a staccato command and staccato applause. What do you think these two terms mean?*

ORCHESTRA SECTIONS

Lots of different instruments play in an orchestra. In fact, sometimes the stage looks very crowded! If you look carefully, you'll see that the musicians are sitting with other musicians who play the same instrument: The violins sit with the violins, the trombones sit with the trombones, and so on. If you look even more carefully, you'll see that the symphony orchestra is divided into four sections:

Strings

Woodwinds

Brass

Percussion

Just remember:

Sitters **W**atch **B**abies **P**lay.

Swans **W**ill **B**ite **P**eople.

SINGING VOICES

Musical pieces written for singing voices generally divide the voices into four parts, from highest voice to lowest.

Soprano

Alto

Tenor

Bass

Think of the parts like this:

Singers **A**lways **T**each **B**reathing.

Singers **A**lways **T**alk **B**oldly.

If you don't care about the order of the voices, you can spell **STAB.**